Satan, I Serve You Notice

CHIVON

authorHOUSE®

AuthorHouse™
1663 Liberty Drive
Bloomington, IN 47403
www.authorhouse.com
Phone: 833-262-8899

Published by AuthorHouse 08/10/2020

ISBN: 978-1-7283-6948-8 (sc)
ISBN: 978-1-7283-6949-5 (e)

Library of Congress Control Number: 2020914603

Print information available on the last page.

Dedication

This book is dedicated to my wonderful and supportive husband, who was my closest friend. To my unforgettable parents, who made it all possible.

To my children, Adrian and Valerie, my joy and pain. My son is a constant reminder that I can do all things through Christ. My daughter is my Elizabeth; every time I'm around her, my purpose leaps.

To my brother and my sisters, who helped mold me into the lady I am. Thanks for giving me your precious time and attention.

To my great inspirations who never gave up on me— Martha Barnwell, Dr. Shirley Fennell, Pat Newby, Connie Rollins, Tina Ross, Dr. Laura, and Linda Townsend. In the beauty field, Mrs. Williams, Mrs. Iris Tryon, and Mr. Robert Ivory.

To every client of Moore's Salon & Beauty Supply, Peaches and Cream Hair Studio, and the Private Hair Doctor Studio, who lived through many of the testimonies in this book. I love you all. Thank you for being a vital part of my life.

Contents

Preface

Why write a book like this? Will anyone read it? Hasn't enough been written about Satan? How long will this book be? Will anyone recommend it? Will this book become an invitation for critics to launch attacks against me?

I could go on allowing the questions to build a wall of intimidation, but as always, I choose to go with my heart and continue to write. But in order for me to begin and then complete this book I must have a driving passion otherwise my life is much too busy to engage. When I thought of what this book could do for readers like you, and excitement bubbled up in me.

When I write, I imagine my readers and what they are going through as they plan their days and set goals for the future. To get ahead in life, we have to prepare for inevitable storms and remember that they don't last forever. Winter, spring, summer and fall come and go, and unemployment and other crises are not under our control, but they too are seasonal. Some people commit suicide when they think their lives are never going to change; people generally don't change unless they have to. When your doctor tells you that you'll die if you continue smoking, you start changing. Crises will change you; they can teach you to prepare for the future.

I had to deal with evil spirits when I was growing up, To get free of them, I had to learn the truth about them because the facts change but the truth remain the same and will set you free. The devil is not a problem if you know the truth about him. He has tricks and strategies; he comes to steal, kill and destroy. He and his demons want a place in your life, but they should have no place in your life. You engage in spiritual warfare when you deal with the devil.

In 2000, a calm voice said to me, "Go to Seguin to take care of your dad," but at first, I didn't pay attention to that voice. I had just purchased my first house and was working as a hair stylist in my five-station salon and was renting out the other four booths. I was busy saving to better my life. But every time my dad came from Seguin to Houston, he would say to my sisters and me, "I'm not getting any younger. One of you girls needs to come to Seguin to take over things before I die."

I didn't think about going; I was in a good spot in life. I had just returned home from Alaska, where I worked with Governor Sheffield conducting hair-weaving seminars in the beauty schools for salon owners. I was content at church, content with my day job at Metro Lift, and was working part time at Headliner Salon with Tina Knowles, Beyonce's mother. Tina and I talked about opening a salon in Alaska; I would manage the place until we found someone to run it, and I would return after that. I was also saving up for a car. I didn't want to give up all that I had going for me, so I told my sisters that one of them needed to go care for Dad in Seguin, but none of them wanted to uproot themselves and families and move to a small town way out in the country.

But that voice kept telling me to go take care of my dad; it said that if I did, I would receive a blessing at the end of the year. That went on for weeks. By the time Dad came from Seguin for another visit, I had come to my senses kinda like the Prodigal Son did. I had visions of the blessing—maybe a large pot of gold. I told Dad that I would go to Seguin after the school year ended; at that time, I was attending ministry school.

When school was out, I moved to Seguin though my mother cried about that; she didn't want me leaving all I had worked so hard for. She said, "You'll never make the money there that you make here." I told her that the Spirit of the Lord had told me several times to go. Besides, I started having problems with my day job, so I thought it was time for me to step out in faith. I told my mother that I would come visit on the weekends, when I had my ministry classes. I had ten months before graduation, and mother was so excited and proud of my being in ministry school, but she didn't get to see me graduate. On December 12, 2002, a year after I moved to Seguin, I got a call from my sister, Erma, that mother had passed.

I hurried back to Houston and handled the funeral arrangements just as mother raised me to do. After the funeral, I returned to Seguin still in a daze and in tears at my mother's death; I wanted to wake up from this nightmare. It wasn't the same traveling to Houston on the weekends, so I earned my degree by mail.

In September 2005, two years later, word came that Hurricane Katrina was on its way. I told my sisters that they should come to Seguin for shelter. They weren't able to come right away because everyone in Houston was trying to leave at the same time. Cars ran out of gas on the highways and were blocking whole lanes.

What do you do when everything collapses? How do you prepare yourself for drastic changes in your life? How do you recover when life blindsides you? What do you do when you are driven by fear?

Continue reading and these questions will be answered.

About My Life

This book is about a girl who was trying to control her dreams as well as her health challenges year after year until the day she found out she had had the antidote all along.

She grew up in Houston, the daughter of Ernest Bibbs and Amelitha Brownlow. She has one brother and six sisters, and she attended Bruce Elementary and then Abraham Lincoln High her junior year; she graduated from Forest Brook High School.

Her first job was in the Galleria Mall at Farrell's Ice Cream Parlor during her senior year, and after graduating, she worked at Dresser Industries as a typist for two years. She attended Franklin Beauty School and received her certificate and license to operate. Evelyn, her sister, wanted her to work for another salon before working with her, so she went to Command Performance Hair Salon, where she gained product knowledge and attended

Pivot Point cutting classes. She was living out a number of her dreams.

She enjoys working out, modeling, singing, styling hair, designing clothes, and spending time with family and with the Holy Spirit. Her dad was a soft-spoken but very motivational person. He would wake the house up with the aroma of fluffy pancakes and bacon and eggs.

Her mother was the prayer warrior in the family. Her favorite snack still today is cinnamon rolls with bologna and cheese and chocolate milk. Her mother gave her and her siblings one job to do—take care of the baby. She didn't experience much of an outside life, but her parents made sure everything she needed and most of what she wanted was available.

She was born with the glory of God in her life. At conception, not at birth, God gave her a great mind and great looks. She was raised in a disciplined environment. She went to bed and got up at certain times, and on Saturdays, her mother would teach her things she needed to know.

She started her first fashion show in 1980 working with full-figured women she named Hot Flash Models. During the fashion show, she would perform as Diana Ross or Sade or Whitney Houston; everyone knew her for her very successful fashion shows. "What's Hot and

What's Not" is still used in her salon today. (Thanks, Tina!)

Her life is everything she ever needed but nothing she ever wanted; however, she knows all things work together even when they don't make sense. She thinks that we learn to get what we need and learn from others that if we believe we can, we can. She knows life isn't fair, but she's happy to wake up every day and enjoy her loved ones all over again and be a blessing for others. She likes giving hugs and smiles to others and telling them she loves them.

She says that no one is in charge of our lives but us, that God gave us life to enjoy, so we should enjoy it. She believes we can live abundant lives free of shame if we stop letting the devil tell us that we are the only one; we have to trust God and exercise our faith especially when we are engaged in spiritual combat.

Introduction

God inspired me to write this book so I could help readers live victorious lives and walk in the power of God. My daughter, Valerie, who is my prophet, wanted me to home school her after spring break, and the week before spring break was over, the coronavirus exploded and is now all over the world making home schooling a necessity. Every time I'm around her, my sense of purpose takes a big leap.

I wrote this book as one very long chapter, but my daughter showed me how to break it up into chapters, glory be to God! This book explains how to minister to others and exercise spiritual authority, and it also deals with Satan and his demons, what everyone needs to know about spiritual forces.

Throughout life, we have to learn how to overcome Satan and serve notice on him and his demons. Strongholds are inaccurate thinking patterns that operate outside the truth. For example, we might feel ashamed of ourselves based on something we have done, but that is the work of Satan, who wants us to feel incapable and unworthy of having an intimate relationship with God; he wants to control our minds and actions.

We walk in the flesh but do not war in the flesh; our weapons are not carnal but spiritual. God will pull down the strongholds we face, take captive everything that exalts itself above him, and make us obedient to Christ. Whether you are Christian or not, you still have to deal with Satan, the prince of ignorance and darkness. In this book, you will experience the power and authority we all have over demonic spirits. God has already equipped us to handle any situation we face; he wants us to be confident and bold enough to deal with Satan and his evil ways. James 4:7 says, "Submit yourselves therefore to God. Resist the devil and he will flee from you."

God has given us the Bible as a roadmap for life. On the day we were born, demons were assigned to us to attack our assignments. These demons know our every move and have strategies to make us fail in our journeys. You've heard that sticks and stones can break our bones but words will never hurt us, but that's a lie; words can attack us. Words spoken out of turn can break a relationship while words spoken in due season can bring joy.

God has equipped us to be confident and bold in the face of the devil. The Holy Spirit will lead us to the place of understanding so we can be strengthened. We will look back at what we have been through and realize that our experiences have prepared us to be where we are now; the Lord orders our footsteps.

We have authority over the devil. When we do something by faith, heaven will back us up. God gives us information as we grow in wisdom and on a need-to-know basis; he knows we will be tested and fall short, but he wants us to stay focused. I always told my mother what the enemy wanted me to do such as getting in the clothes washer and take a ride. A demonic spirit said no one will know, but the Spirit of God warned me about the danger; the devil lost that contest.

I've learned never to respond permanently to temporary problems. I've learned that all I shared this with couldn't understand me because they couldn't visualize it, so they couldn't believe it. This is a faith walk; this is my promise when God speaks specifically to me. You can't tell people who don't know your assignment unless they have gone through similar situations.

People will pray for you as long as you are in need, but the moment you get a breakthrough, jealousy will set in and they will begin to criticize you and try to make you feel ashamed when they should be happy for your believing that their blessings are just around the corner.

Chapter 1

Satan, You Have No Authority over Me

Power is a natural ability, a dynamic energy, a force, but authority is the legal right to exercise that power. A person with authority is more dangerous than a person with power. The devil isn't afraid of your power, but God gave you your authority, the authority of Jesus, and authority will eat power for lunch.

Moses showed Pharaoh the power he commanded when he threw his staff down and it became a snake. Pharaoh showed his power when his priest threw down a staff and it became a snake. Moses showed Pharaoh his authority when his snake ate Pharaoh's snake.

Your authority—personal and divine—will empower you. You exercise your personal authority, which you were born with, but you have to submit to divine authority for it to function properly. Most people think that their personal gifts are enough; they can sing and preach, but that's only their personal authority, a gift from God. Birds fly, but we don't; that ability was not given to us. If we try to do something we're not authorized to do, it could kill us. The devil wants to kill us, but he cannot kill what he did not create and cannot stop what he didn't start.

These demonic spirits had me believing that I could commit suicide and that it would be okay, that nobody would care. But when you begin to think about the people who love you and what it would do to them if you died, you rethink your situation. Knowing that others love you and that you love them is most important. Satan knows what and whom to choose to get your attention, so stay focused in your lane and keep driving.

They were on a mission to attack me. I had a terrible cough and was running a fever; I saw evil spirits ascending and descending the curtains in my room and trying to grab me. I was too weak to move, but I was covered with anointed oil, the blood of Jesus. I still had to speak the Word of God and rebuke the devil. My mother always rubbed anointed oil on me and placed her prayer cloth on me. The evil spirits wanted to catch me off guard, but victory was mine.

The evil spirits came back another time and tried to suffocate me while I was sleeping, I screamed, "No! No!"

I was fighting to breathe; my mother entered my room and touched me, and I woke up. I asked her if she had heard me screaming, and she said no. I told her what had happened, and she reassured me that I was covered by her prayer cloth and need not worry.

I wanted to take control of my dreams, so I asked my mother to wake me up in fifteen minutes just in case I wouldn't get out of my dream in time. That time, I was ready for them. They showed me lots of money, and I grabbed as much as I could; I wanted to show my mother what I took from the wicked, but when I woke up and opened my hand, there was nothing to see.

While sleeping, I came in contact with the demon spirits again; they attacked my mind, and I struggled and gasped for air. I screamed, but again, no one heard me, so I called on the one I knew would never leave me—Jesus, who casts down high thoughts that exhaust themselves against the Word of God and brings every thought into obedience with him.

Finally, my mother did wake me, but that time, I felt powerful. I felt good knowing that I was not distracted by Satan's strategies. Satan knows you are too smart to do something wrong, so he focuses on getting you to do something good because when you do, you think you've done something right; that's one of Satan's tricks.

My brother was the only one who understood me because he was having very similar encounters with evil spirits. He was prideful, so he didn't tell anyone—he simply acted it out. He would jump off things thinking he could fly, and he kept hurting himself; one day, he cut his arm very badly and went to the hospital, but once he was out of the hospital, he was at it again. He tried crossing a freeway too soon or too late and was struck by a car and then a truck. He was rushed to the hospital, where he died a week later.

We have to stand firm against the tricks and schemes of the devil, who tries to get us to see things from his perspective and to draw us from God, but the only power Satan has is the power we give him. These spirits won't stop. They get into your thoughts and make you think the way they think. If all you see is what you see, you don't see all there is to see; the invisible affects the visible I know from experience seeing what happened to my brother but not quite understanding it all.

When we got sick, Mother would spend weeks nursing us back to health with home remedies and prayer. She would place her anointed prayer cloth on us under our clothes and rub her blessed oil on us, a safety measure she strongly believed in.

During Bible school before services, there would be testimony time. I wanted to tell others what had been happening to me as my testimony, but the demonic spirits would tell me not to speak in the church. Satan knew that I would always tell my mother everything, so he tricked me into not giving my testimony. Satan does everything he does only because we told him it was okay to do so. He needs our bodies and minds to express himself to others, but he needs our permission to take over our minds and bodies. Satan will play with our thinking system by having us believe that people wouldn't understand us. Demons would tell me, "Just tell God—he already knows, and he is the only one who needs to know." These spirits convinced me to keep quiet. I thought if God already knows, that's all that matters, but they kept showing up because they knew that they could hold me back if I kept quiet, but I told my mother everything; there weren't any secrets between us. Satan knew he had no authority over me, but Satan knew that the moment I had the chance, I would tell my mother and eventually give my testimony.

Before the service started at our church, there would be thirty minutes of testimony, and my mother would always join in then. One Sunday, she convinced me that I had a testimony. Someone testified to receiving an unexpected check, and another testified to being saved from a potential head-on collision by the grace of God. After all that they and others testified to, I had hope that I could testify to my demonic attacks, but speaking out at church took me some time because the evil spirits had some kind of control over me that had me thinking I was doing the right thing by not testifying.

I would lie to Mother to keep from going to church by saying I didn't have stockings to wear, or that my dress was dirty, or that I felt sick, but my excuses didn't work with her; she said I needed to have the Holy Spirit. At church, we would lift up our hands and say, "Jesus! Jesus!" and I would speak in tongues. You get the Holy Spirit by calling on the name of Jesus; that causes demons to tremble, yokes to be destroyed, and burdens to be lifted.

The saints knew the power behind Jesus's name; if doctors told them they had cancer, they would tell them to save that diagnosis for someone who doesn't know Jesus. When you have the Holy Spirit, you can look at any demon and say, "God gave me the power to tread on serpents and scorpions and not be harmed by any deadly thing! I can lay hands on myself and heal myself!"

Around that time, I stopped being foolish and began to confess God's will over my life. I decided that I would live, not die. My mother told me what I needed to do to keep from going through my health challenge, but it wasn't until I remembered how the demonic spirits moved up and down the curtains in my room that I began to activate my faith. Faith is believing in what you don't see, and I believed in her daily. As Mother rubbed my entire body with blessed oil, I was too weak to move, but I appreciated the care and time she put in to keep my health and strength up, and I never forgot that I had dominion over the demons. I never forgot how those evil spirits paused and hid behind the curtains. When my mother pulled the curtains back, opened the window, and started praying, those demonic spirits left.

During the last year I went through this health challenge, it wasn't till I was so sick, on the edge of my death bed that time, that I didn't just hear Mother—I also obeyed her. And as the seasons changed, I knew when to drink lemon tea and eat vegetables and tomato soup with crackers. I felt better. I have not had a health challenge like that in decades. The next chapter will tell you how I overcame it all.

Chapter 2

Satan, You Have No Power over Me

Our worlds are formed by our words. Life and death are in the power of the tongue, which can cause great destruction in our lives. If you discipline yourself in prayer, God will eventually bring you to a place of spiritual power.

I always wanted to be a praying person like my mother; I'd heard that God would give you just what you ask for, so I was going to write down my vision plainly and specifically. I asked God to send me someone who knew more about him so I could know him better. I met a man of God who was in the church—tall, dark, and handsome. I thought to myself, *This is good. I got what I asked for.* As they say, you have not because you ask not. We don't look in between to see the bad; we just focus on the good. God sent this man to me to help me pray, but

I didn't see it that way. I chose to get married. I chose to have his baby. I chose to go through destruction.

To get to the place I wanted to be, I had to go through hell's storms, but it was a learning situation that strengthened me to handle any situation God was preparing me for. I needed to stay focused on what I asked God for because once I got off focus, I opened the door to the devil and gave him the right of way to do his evil. Remember that the devil will always come in disguise.

I had the power to tread on serpents and scorpions and all the powers of the enemy, but I lost sight of that. Satan had power over me because I gave my power to him, but he doesn't have authority over me. When we take control of our minds, we take control of our thinking and don't allow anyone else to do that; knowing who we are makes us bold. The devil doesn't mind our being religious, but he will find a way to grab our attention and turn something good into something bad as if by magic. He will try to convince us that his thoughts are ours. Colossians 2:18 tells us that we should let no one beguile us; what doesn't kill us makes us stronger. God loves you because of who God is.

I [insert your name here] declare that I have the grace I need for today. I am full of power, strength, and determination. Nothing I face will be too much for me. I will overcome every obstacle, outlast every challenge, and come through every difficulty. I declare that it is not too late to accomplish everything God has placed in my heart. I have not missed my window of opportunity.

God has moments of favor in my future. He is preparing me right now because he is about to release a special grace to help me accomplish that dream. This is my time, this is my moment, and I received it today.

If all you see is what you see, you don't see all there is to be seen; the invisible affects the visible, so stand firm against the schemes and strategies of the devil, who doesn't want you to know his schemes. The devil wants you to think of him as a comical horned figure in a red jumpsuit holding a pitchfork, not a deceptive schemer who can trick you.

The Bible say that the snake is one of the most crafty reptiles; Satan used one to deceive Adam and Eve. Demons need bodies to do their work. Satan schemes to trick us; he doesn't want us to see him for what he really is, so he comes looking like something else to get us to move away from the protective covering of God as he did Adam and Eve. Satan tries to trick us into seeing things from his perspective so he can draw us away from God, but the only power he and his demons have is the power we give them.

We are told they have been defeated, but why then are we not winning? They do everything they do because we gave them permission to use us to express themselves. If our lives are hell, that's because we gave the devil the okay to make our lives hell by giving our minds and bodies to him so he can work his evil. We should not give Satan and his demons permission to tell us how we will live mentally; we must stand firm because we have already won a victory over him.

Just like an umbrella can protect us from the rain, which is otherwise all around us, God can protect us from evil even if it is all around us. The devil will try to entice us to step out from under God's protection, but our faith in God will be our source of strength to stay where we are—strong in the Lord. Colossians 2:10 says we are complete in Jesus, who has rendered the devil powerless; he can't beat us with power, only with deception that looks like power. If someone pointed a gun at you, you would be terrified, but if you discovered that the gun had no bullets, that would change how you viewed your situation. Satan only looks like he has firepower, but he is no longer in control.

Colossians 2:15 says that when Jesus died on the cross, he conducted a victory parade in heavenly places; he declared Satan and his demons defeated in the spiritual realm. Jesus declared that Satan can whip us only if we give him permission to do so.

Don't be anxious about anything but in everything by prayer and supplication with thanksgiving let your request be made known to God and the peace of God which surpasses all understanding will guard your hearts and your minds in Christ Jesus. (Philippians 4:6–7)

You should not fear them for it is the Lord your God who fights for you. (Deuteronomy 3:22)

I command the powers of the enemy to be broken off you and your loved ones, your home, your ministry, and your relationships, hallelujah! They are broken off my body, my life, my children, my marriage, my spouse, my business, and my practice. I decree and declare that God has freed me from the evil control of the enemy. I command every evil attachment to be broken. I take authority over the spirits of doubt, fear, terror, confusion, unbelief, sin, and intimidation.

I release myself from the strongholds of the enemy and the evil forces that bombard my mind. Evil spirits, you have no power over me. Satan, I know you are after my thoughts, but so is God. He knows we're the real deal.

What we think about comes out of our mouths; it's the power of suggestion, and to God be the glory in the name of Jesus. God, Psalm 143:8–10 causes me to hear your loving-kindness. I know the way I should walk, and

13

I lift up my soul to you. Deliver me, O Lord, from my enemies. Teach me to do your will, and lead me to the land of uprightness.

We have to take authority over our mouths. I believe that God is stronger in my life; I believe that things are changing as I speak. You won't say it because you don't feel it at times, but your words can bring manifestation, so grab it and put it in your heart. I cancel every negative word that's been spoken against your will for my life, God, in the name of Jesus. Lord, give me understanding and the conviction of the Holy Spirit; give me grace to handle all my situations, and help me be bold and strong in them. Whoever Jesus sets free is free indeed. Free me and those I speak over; let us never lose.

Never cry for those who hurt you; just smile and thank them for giving you a chance to find others better than them in Jesus's name. Something has to come to an end in your life. It's not the end that destroys people, and it's not the beginning that gives people hope; it's the time in between that destroys them.

Chapter 3

Spiritual Warfare

To deal with spiritual warfare, you have to understand the history of spiritual conflict. God made the first move when he created the angels, but then, Lucifer rebelled against God and took a third of the angels with him. God countered that by creating man in his image a little lower than the angels. Satan rebelled against that by getting Adam and Eve to turn the earth over to his control. God countered that move by the redemptive covering for Adam and Eve so they could return to fellowship with him.

Of course, Satan tried to counter that by getting Cain to kill Abel to cut off the godly line. God countered that move with the birth of Seth so men could call on the name of the Lord again. Satan tried to counter that move through the birth of Nimrod, who built the civilizations of Babylon and Assyria. People gathered at the Tower of Babel to build the region to defend themselves against

God, but God countered that move by declaring that Abraham would create a nation of people who would obey him. Satan countered that move by getting God's people trapped in Egypt, but God got Moses to tell Pharaoh, "Let my people go!"

The Old Testament is filled with moves and countermoves. There were four hundred silent years between the end of the Old Testament and the beginning of the New Testament, which says in Matthew 1:16 that Mary gave birth to Jesus after God said in essence, "I'm tired of this, man! Let me go down there to take care of this myself." God became man in the person of Jesus Christ, whom Satan tried to tempt in the wilderness and had crucified. That's when God made his final move; Jesus rose from the dead and confirmed our victory over Satan.

I will share with you how you can use the final move: Ephesians 6:10 tells us,

> Be strong in the Lord put on the full armor of God your struggle is not against flesh and blood but against principalities and powers in the world forces of this Darkness against the spiritual forces of wickedness in Heavenly places.

People are not the problem we think they are because they are what we see, taste, and feel, but whatever is going wrong in our lives is not due to flesh and blood but due to what's going on in the spiritual realm. Whatever is happening in the world of our five senses, our flesh and blood, was created in an unseen world. If we can't navigate that world, we can't fix this world. Our blessings are in the heavenly realm, where spiritual warfare started.

Deuteronomy 31:6 tells us that we should be strong and courageous, not fearful. God is with us and will not forsake us as he promised us. We just have to walk in faith not because we've seen someone else do that but because his Word said we should walk in faith, and God does not lie. We are a royal priesthood, the head, not the tail. We proceed through life as first-class believers.

We can choose life or death, blessings or curses. We live in a world that is driven by decisions; love and hate are driven by decisions. We are helped by the Holy Spirit and are hindered by Satan; two forces are tugging on us. There are a lot of things we're gonna lose in life, but we should never lose our ability to think for ourselves.

I mentioned my brother, Wendell, who was always getting hurt by his antics such as jumping off the washing machine thinking he could fly. One time, he jumped off something holding an umbrella thinking he would float down, but he twisted his ankle and ended up in the hospital. He was in the hospital for a week after he was hit by that car and truck I mentioned. My mother and I visited him in the hospital until he took his last breath.

After that, my mother would wake up because she thought she had heard Wendell crying as he did when he was an infant. She heard him call out to her and others in the family, and we heard him playing. It became very cold in the house, and I felt his presence under my covers; it was as if he were trying to tell us that he was okay and that we should not worry; he didn't want Mother crying herself to sleep.

We never heard him or felt his presence again. I believe he wanted to spend one last time with us in the Spirit. My mother would always ask God how he could have let him die. I wanted Mother not to cry, so I would tell her that maybe God took him home so he wouldn't keep hurting himself.

My mother started reading a big, black book she said was the Bible. She read in Exodus that God was a jealous God, and she concluded that she had loved her son so much that God had taken him, that she should never love anyone more than she loved God, a jealous God.

The god of this world, the devil, is active and wants to get hold of our promise in the earthly realm to get us to make bad choices. A battle is raging between the forces of good and evil, and in it, God is a jealous God. It wasn't God but the demonic spirit who enters our minds to get us to think like him so we will destroy ourselves, but he is so dumb; the victory is already ours.

When I was in high school, I learned that one of my classmates was secretly smoking pot. I told her that she was missing something in her life—Jesus. I'd ask her to attend church with me, but she didn't want to. I wanted to find out what she was getting from smoking, so one time, I took a puff, and I saw the heavens before me as if I were looking down from heaven. That was the first and last time I took a puff. I never said anything to her about church again. One day, however, she asked me about going to church, and when she did, she joined church and got rid of the drugs. Today, she is a member of T. D. Jakes's church and is living in a nice home and driving a nice car. Praise God, hallelujah!

Around that time, my aunt Gwen was in the hospital; she had been diagnosed with breast cancer. She didn't want to say anything to the family; she went for weeks not talking, just doing sign language. Mother was so hurt about that and the prospect of losing her sister. I couldn't imagine what my aunt was going through; she had two sons, one in college and the other in high school. When Aunt Gwen passed away, her older son came to take care of his brother in Fort Worth, where he graduated from high school and then moved to Houston to be close to us.

My sister Karen always told me that if anything ever happened to her, she wanted me to take care of her daughter, and I would always say okay. When the time came, I did take her in. She graduated from high school, and during her first year in college, she became pregnant, which triggered leukemia in her. The doctors told her that she had to have an abortion to save her life, but she wanted to keep her baby.

During her difficult pregnancy, there were days when she would fall on the floor. She was waiting for a bone marrow transplant, and when she was strong enough for it, she had the procedure done. She produced a video for her daughter so she could see it when she got older.

As time went on, I watched my niece preparing herself for transition. I was proud of her relationship with God and her strength. I watched her faith grow while I was learning more about God's Word myself.

One time, my niece told me that my fiancé was a hypocrite; she said that he was no good and that her spirit had walked around the hospital and saw him chatting with women. She saw my future, but I didn't listen because I believed in God and was sure I had made the right decision about marrying the man, but we did end up divorcing.

My niece had a beautiful girl, five pounds and seven ounces. My niece lived with us for six months and left her mother a lovely baby, but she never came home from the hospital; we celebrated her twenty-first birthday there. My niece took a turn for the worse and went into a coma. The doctors told us that they were going to pull the plug in the morning. I kept on praying for her with all my might.

The next day, it was as if nothing had happened; all was well with her. She told me that she had heard everything the doctors had said about keeping her on the machine till the morning. The doctors said that she was gone, that there was nothing else they could do, but in her secret place, I heard her screaming, "I'm not dead!" I did not stop praying for her.

I learned that those in comas are in an unseen world and can hear others speak. What do you do when it seems God is not near and is not answering your prayers? What do you do when it seems God is not moving in the spiritual realm?

When you are relying on a navigation system to get somewhere, it will warn you when you get off track. I believe that God gave us that time to prepare us but also to help us understand what happens when someone is in a coma and the doctors say there is nothing more they can do. Only God can help in such a situation, not doctors, parents, or even preachers. When no one but God can help you, you don't owe anybody but God.

She wasn't afraid anymore; she came back stronger. A spiritual friend gave her a nice picture that was on the spiritual wall in her room. We couldn't see it, so we asked her to describe it to us. She said it was a girl standing in a grassy yard behind a white fence on a sunny day.

After my divorce, I looked and prayed for someone who knew more about God than I did, someone who would teach me to pray more, and yes, I got what I had asked God for because that sent me down the path I needed to take, and I came out a praying woman.

I hope I've encouraged you to live the life of your dreams because that's possible with God.

Chapter 4

Satan, I Call You Out

Interrupting Satan's plan the devil has a plan for your soul but so does God. The church is no longer becoming; it is a being. The Pentecost represents the fulfillment of the church. The Pentecost marks the birth of the church; because of the Holy Spirit, the church is a being. Faith comes by hearing the Word of God. I'm not becoming anything; I am already who God says I am. I'm not becoming blessed because I'm already blessed. I'm not becoming favored because I'm already favored. I'm not becoming healed because I'm already healed.

Every now and then, your mind will play tricks on you and try to make you believe something that's not there is really there. Your mind and the enemy will try to make you believe that God has forgotten about what he said, but what you have been believing in God for is not something that is becoming but that is already here. Praise

God for what you don't see, and don't worry about the things you see, which are temporary. Get your praise on everywhere, not just in church. If you really got a praise deep down inside, you can wake up in the morning and start praising him because he woke you up. Praise him before you leave home no matter where you're going.

When I began writing this book, I would get to the embarrassing parts and stop writing for several months while doing other things, but the urge to write it would always come back and inspire me to continue writing. I prayed that the Holy Spirit would give me the courage to finish this book even when I felt empty. I cried out to God, "What am I here for? I'm not being fed spiritually at church!" I asked the Holy Spirit to lead me to a church so I could use my knowledge and be a blessing. I said, "God, you told me to go to Seguin to take care of my father, which I did. You said I would receive a blessing." He said, "I didn't tell you to go to church or any other place except Seguin. You were doing your will, not mine."

The Holy Spirit told me, "This is what I want you to do—stay home on Sundays finish your book. I will tell you what to do next." I asked, "What will I say to people when they ask why I haven't been to church?" He said, "Tell them I'm your pastor."

After that sunk in, it went well with me a friend started her church and held services on Saturdays, and I thought that was great, no worries about going on Sunday. This was during January 2018. I had just become a widow, and I was dealing with all this at the same time Satan was trying to get me off track.

A friend of mines needed my help moving so she could put her house up for sell on a Sunday, this went on for six months. I attended funeral after funeral, some was on Saturday and others were on Sunday I was thinking If I could spend at least three hours each Sunday writing my book first then I could help every one else, but I decided to take time to myself on Sunday for what I needed to do. When you have a strong vision of your assignment, it will stay on your mind till you finish it. That's one way you will know your calling even if you have an assigned demon that reports to Satan. He still has no authority over you. You sit under the authority of Jesus when you obey the Holy Spirit and let him guide you to the truth.

Things happen all the time; it's how we handle those things that's important. Satan will try to distract us with empty promises—"You can write later. It's going to be okay." Satan just wants us out of his way so he'll do everything to hurt us, and when we play with sin, sin play with us. That's why it's important for us to pray in all things; we should not wait till the battle is over before we learn about Satan's strategies. Proverb 14:12 tells us that there is a way that seems right to a man, but it will end in spiritual death. Keep your distance from people who lead you astray if you don't want to be led astray; always ask yourself, *What if…?*

You might think that crack will not hurt you, but you'll find yourself losing everything you have including your future if you continue thinking that. You know the devil is a liar, so don't listen to him at all. Hebrews 5:14 tells us that we are to eat spiritual meat if we want to discern between good and evil.

Years ago, my son told me, "Mom, you said the Tooth Fairy is real, but I know that's not true. My tooth came out last night, and I put it under my pillow. This morning, it was still there, and there wasn't any money!" I was so embarrassed! Then he asked me about Santa Claus, as if he didn't know the answer and I decided not to lie about that; I said, "I'm Santa Claus, dear." So when I took him to see Santa Claus in the mall, he sat on his lap, and when Santa Claus asked him what he wanted for Christmas, my son pulled the man's beard down and laughed at him: "You're not Santa!" His knowing the truth took away some of the fun and anticipation of Christmas, but it did teach me to tell him the truth, and I did the same with my daughter. The truth is eternal. It will set you free!

Do you know how depressed the devil is when he fails to get you to sin? Death came alive through the disobedience of Adam and Eve, but righteousness can save many. Let the devil know that you are aware of his secret. He's all around you and trying to sabotage you as he did Adam and Eve, but he is powerless over you unless you give in to his temptations and fail to have faith in God and his goodness. If you sin, quickly confess it to God, who with Jesus's shed blood will cleanse you.

People are often unreasonable, selfish, and rational, but we should forgive them anyway; if we do, we will win some unfaithful friends for Christ and gain some genuine enemies, but forgiveness is a virtue. Others can destroy overnight what we have spent years creating, but we should not stop creating. We should give all we have even though it will never be enough. Give your all any way. It's all between us and God, not between us and others.

The devil cannot force us to sin, but he will try to make us think in a way that seems right but ultimately results in wrong. As I said, the devil is not a problem when we know the truth. We should thank God for every time the devil tries to attack us; we should praise God and give him glory for the things we don't see because what we do see is temporary.

The enemy has tried to stop me many times but has failed. He tried to attack my body, but I'm still here. He tried to attack my mind, but I've finished this book. He tried to attack my children, but no weapon formed against me will prosper. I give him a failing grade because his attacks against me have failed!

Printed in the United States
By Bookmasters